Juan Soto

How Juan Soto Became The Most Exciting Player In The MLB

By

Jackson Carter

Copyright © 2022

Table of Contents

Table of Contents

Legal Notes

A Special Athlete For A Special Sport

What Makes Juan Soto Special?

Growing Up

Born Into The Game

A New Dominican Star

School, Family, Ball

Learning The Game

Proving Himself: The Minor Leagues

The Next Level

The Big Show

The Biggest Games Yet

The World Series

Moving On

2021 And Beyond

What's Next For Juan Soto?

More From Jackson Carter Biographies

Other Works By Jackson Carter Biographies

Legal Notes

Juan Soto is meant for entertainment and educational use only. All attempts have been made to present factual information in an unbiased context.

© 2022 Broad Base Publishing

All rights reserved. No portion of this book may be reproduced in any form without permission from the publisher, except as permitted by U.S. copyright law. For permissions contact:

BroadBasePublishing@Gmail.com

A Special Athlete For A Special Sport

There are far too many people who think that baseball is an easy sport to play.

Because of its slower speed or its simple premise, some people think that all you need to do to be good at playing the game is stand straight, aim for the ball, and hit it as hard as you can when it comes your way.

Most people's experience with baseball came when they were participating in T-Ball or little league as children—nothing that really required more than some fun in the sun and a little bit of sweat. They think that baseball pales in comparison to the difficulty levels of games such as soccer, basketball, football, or even golf.

But it is evident that people who think like that do not know much about the game. Baseball is so much more than holding a bat in your hand and attempting to swing with all your might when a ball comes your way. No, there are so many complicated, complex, difficult, and layered levels to the game. There is a reason why millions of people watch in awe as superior athletes take to the diamond and win games, series, and championships.

There is just no denying that baseball is a tricky, hard game. There might be many games in one season—more than 180 in fact—but that doesn't take away from the intensity and the difficulty associated with America's pastime.

Therefore, the men you see making a career in baseball are beyond talented athletes. They understand how to master a game, which is about more than just a ball and a bat. They know that the game is about strategy, strength, intelligence, stamina, and much more. So much goes into play when performing well at baseball and the best of the best understand that.

Juan Soto is one of the best of the best. He has only been playing the game for a few years, but he is now understood to be one of the very greatest to suit up in the uniform and cleats. Since joining the MLB in 2018, Soto has raced through the rankings of the Washington Nationals to not only become a breakout star but an All-Star, two-time All-MLB First Team, All-MLB Second Team, two-time Silver Slugger Award, National League batting champion, and, best of all, a World Series champion.

He's done all of this in just a few years, and all before the age of 24.

Soto is indeed recognized as one of the strongest, most accomplished, and most talented baseball players alive. But his ride to the top wasn't always easy. He's been long considered too young to be so good and has had to push back against a lot of criticisms. He has also had to suffer and push through injuries that have derailed his talent and his chances of going far in the league.

Soto has always wanted to thrive in the game since he was a youth. He plays with the sort of energy you see in someone who lives and breathes the sport and whose entire life revolves around it. Soto isn't playing only for himself. Instead, he is playing for a country that roots him on, a family that has always supported him, and the young man he once was—a young man who watched baseball in awe, hoping to someday conquer other teams like the heroes of his youth.

Soto is now known for a lot of things: his skill, personality, and success. No matter the team you root for or what you think of Soto's personality, you have to admit that he is one special player.

What Makes Juan Soto Special?

It's hard to exactly pinpoint why Soto is such a valuable and incredible baseball player. The fact of the matter is that he has so many positive assets about him. There are quite a few attributes that make him such an attractive player, not only to fans of the Washington Nationals but also to fans of the game in general.

If you want to really stand out while playing in the MLB, you need to have more than talent. You need to have an attitude and personality that really shine. And there is no doubt that Soto most certainly has those in spades.

But let's talk about talent because when you add up Soto and his accomplishments, even in the short career he's had, you see something truly special. At the end of the 2021 season, for example, Soto has the fifth-highest career walk rate and the tenth-highest career on-base percent amongst batters with at least 2,000 appearances at the plate. These numbers show that Soto is the type of player who can get on base again and again, regardless of how he gets there. He is renowned for his great plate discipline. In other words, Juan is known to be someone who will put his head down and do what it takes to get his cleats on a base.

And now let's talk about the personality that goes along with the skills. Juan is a fun player to watch and not just because he has what it takes to get himself on base often. He entertains the fans in the stands and those at home, and that's a huge part of his appeal too. For example, the "Soto Shuffle" is a routine in which Soto frequently hops, taps his leg, swings his hips, wipes the ground with a broad arc of his leg, swings his hips, or lowers himself into a squat while glancing at the pitcher. It's quite a show and it fires up the fans at home and at the field.

"He'll swing his hips or spread his legs or sweep his feet or shimmy his shoulders or lick his lips or squeeze his, um, junk, sometimes all at once" as one ESPN journalist put it. As you can imagine, it's an interesting thing to see in the middle of a baseball game. "To get in the minds of the pitchers because sometimes they get scared," Soto claims he started the ritual in the lower levels of the baseball world when he was an up-and-coming athlete hoping to make the major leagues.

To some, the Soto Shuffle is fun and humorous. To others, it's too much. Pitcher Miles Mikolas of the St. Louis Cardinals didn't care for it and saw it as being braggadocious. He replied to Soto's antics in Game 1 of the 2019 National League Championship Series by grasping his own crotch after retiring Soto on a groundout. Shortly after that, Soto reeled it and refrained from doing his signature dance during games. Still, his personality, fun attitude, and love of the game still shine during every match-up.

Let's touch upon his skills once again. Again and again, Soto has shown that he is not only talented on the field but supremely intelligent too. He has an understanding of the game—and his playstyle—that has taken him to a level that few professional athletes reach. You can see it in the way he holds himself at the batter's box. Soto has a "two-strike approach" wherein he lifts his grip on the bat handle and assumes a broader, lower stance in the batter's box that is sometimes referred to as a crouch. Even with two strikes, he is renowned for his ability to drive the ball to all parts of the field and it all starts with the way he stands, holds the bat, and sizes up his pitching opponents.

The proof is in the numbers, and Juan's numbers have grown increasingly more and more impressive throughout his few years in the MLB. Soto hit 23 home runs to left field, 23 to center, plus another 23 to right field during the course of his MLB career at the end of the 2020 season.

He's fun to watch, he's intelligent, and he's versatile. Juan has shown a preference for playing on the right field, which is where he primarily played during his brief minor league career even though he was nominated for a Gold Glove Award as a left fielder following the 2019 season. Being a left fielder was just a natural fit for him and it was where he was most comfortable. Additionally, it was where he found an awful lot of success for himself and the team as a whole.

But one of the things that set Soto apart is that he doesn't have to stay in one place and he can find great success and victories from all over the diamond. In late 2020, the Nationals' head coaching staff decided to start using Soto as the right fielder to start their games. For many athletes, this would be a huge undertaking and could throw them off their games and take a long time for adjustment. There would be a lot of trials and errors and mistakes during that adjustment period. That wasn't the case for Juan Soto. He didn't just do satisfactory in this new position; he positively thrived. In fact, by 2021, he was the team's regular right fielder.

As you can see, Juan Soto is not your everyday type of baseball player. He has a natural skill, talent, intelligence, drive, and personality that has attracted fans from all over the world. He is playing like a man possessed, a man meant to play the game, a man who will settle for nothing less than the very best.

Juan Soto is simply one of the best, most exciting, and most beloved baseball players alive today. And his road to the big leagues was filled with a lot of effort, a lot of setbacks, and a lot of challenges. He may be just 23 years old, but Soto has been through a lot in just over the 20 years he's been alive.

Growing Up

To understand what baseball means to Juan Soto and how and why it has shaped his life and had such an impact on him, you have to first understand what it means to the people of the Dominican Republic.

Baseball isn't just a big deal to the people of the DR; it's a *huge* deal. And it has been for over a century now. Next to the United States, the Dominican Republic has the highest number of baseball fans and baseball players. It's a national pastime just as it is in the United States. And it's where Juan Soto was born, raised, and fell in love with the game that would change him forever.

Due to the Ten Years' War, many Cuban residents left their country in the 1870s. Many people moved to the Dominican Republic, taking baseball with them. In 1890, the country's professional class of players was created. Nuevo and Ozama were the first clubs. Santo Domingo's Licey club was founded on November 7th, 1907. By the 1930s it became a magnet for talented athletes whose guardians typically worked in sugar mills. American luminaries of the Negro League, notably Satchel Paige, visited the nation in 1937. Rafael Trujillo constructed the main stadium in the middle of the 1950s. A utility infielder named Ozzie Virgil was the first Dominican player to immigrate to the United States to play for Major League Baseball.

Baseball has a significant impact on the Dominican Republic's culture as a whole, in addition to helping to improve ties between the country and the United States. Today, baseball unites baseball fans (old and young) from numerous Spanish-speaking nations and represents a desire and hope for a brighter future for aspiring players. The growth of the game in the DR has also had a significant influence on the economy of the nation as a whole, with training grounds and professional games producing about $1 billion annually.

Most people growing up in the Dominican Republic during the early 1900s all the way until the 1950s were surrounded by baseball. It was quickly becoming one of the most important aspects of the country and its people. Many young people grew up watching the MLB greats of the time and imagining themselves playing in America someday.

Of course, this was a different time when international players were not nearly as common in the US. It just wasn't done as much because baseball was run by a league that was hardly breaking the racial barrier, let alone the international one. It would be years before there would be foreign-born players dominating the league.

But when those players, such as Juan Soto, eventually arrived in the league, they made up for lost time and would stand out and make solid, memorable names for themselves, even against some of the best American players.

Born Into The Game

By the 1990s, the Dominican Republic was still very devoted to the game and they had produced many terrific players who had made the leap from the DR to the US and had become huge professional athletes in the MLB. And it was during that time period that Juan Soto was born into a nation—and family—that absolutely adored baseball and had quite a bit of experience with it too.

Juan Soto, Sr. and Belkis Pacheco were Juan's parents, and he was born in the city of Santo Domingo.

From the very beginning, Juan's young life was filled with baseball and the energy and excitement that surrounds it. That is because Juan's father, Juan Sr., has quite a bit of experience playing baseball himself. Juan Sr. played in Santo Domingo's local men's league. And around the time that his son could walk, Juan Sr. was out in the front yard of his home tossing the baseball around. Even before Juan Soto could talk, he was playing baseball, and he was quickly falling in love with the game.

Juan Sr.'s love of the game didn't just impact and guide Juan Jr. Juan has one younger brother and a sister who is older and they also fell in love with baseball from birth. In fact, when his brother, Elian, becomes eligible in January 2023, he will sign a verbal contract to join the Nationals organization. As you can see, the love of the game was in their veins, their very DNA. Yet, it would be Juan who would take his love of baseball and turn it into more than a hobby but a wildly successful career.

Anyone who knew Juan at a young age predicted that he would become a baseball star in the future. It just felt like something he was destined to do. His talent, even from his youth, was evident during every game he played. After a few years of tossing the ball around with his father in the front yard, Juan had accumulated a slew of skills that would eventually advance, enhance, and evolve into the same techniques and talents that would make him a multi-millionaire and one of the biggest names in the game.

While the talent that Juan had and still has feels natural and born into him, there was something else at play that really impacted the young man and made him into the up-and-coming superstar he would be by his teens. It was his father and his father's love of the game—and support of his son—that put Juan on a path straight to the professional league.

Yes, a major part of Juan's success is due to his dad. Other fathers would simply play ball with their kids and use it as a way to connect and have fun after a long day. While Juan Sr. did that, he also quickly caught on that his son was a natural talent who really could be fostered into something special, something professional, something very successful.

Baseball is a young man's game, especially in the Dominican Republic. The truth is that there aren't many older baseball players in the MLB. That's because the game, despite what some people think, is actually quite physical and not very generous or friendly to those much older than 30. So, if you want to be a professional ball player, you'll have to do that when you're young.

As for Juan, he had to work extra hard if he wanted to be an MLB star because of his location.

A New Dominican Star

In some ways, coming from the Dominican Republic can help young players hoping to make their way to America and the MLB. At the same time, it can also hold a person back and make it harder for that person to have a breakthrough.

It can be great for a young player hoping to break through because the Dominican Republic has become known as a hotbed for great baseball talent for the last several decades. From Pedro Martinez to Sammy Sosa to David Ortiz and more, the DR is a nation that takes great pride in producing spectacular, young, driven, and talented players ready to pour all of themselves into the game.

But that also means that young players coming from the Dominican Republic may be held to an unfair standard. There are many great baseball stars who have come from the island nation, of course, but many of the young prospects coming from there are judged based on their chances of becoming the next big thing. If they don't show a natural, untouched talent similar to Martinez or Sosa, they could be cast away by young scouts.

In other words, people expect the very best form of baseball hopefuls from the Dominican Republic. Anything less than utter perfection and these young guys can be lost in the fray and the hubbub and all the noise of the world of professional sports.

Juan's father was well aware of all of that. How could he not be? Though he was a salesman while his son was diving headfirst into baseball, he was once determined to be a professional ball player too. There was a time in his life when he was playing ball every single day and really did see a chance for himself on the shores of America, playing with a big league team. But as they so often do, those dreams slowly dwindled away and died over the years and Juan Sr. was left with the reality of home life, fatherhood, and the responsibility of putting a roof over his family's head and keeping them fed and happy.

At the end of the day, Juan Sr. had to ask himself if he really had what it took to put it all on the line and make a run at being an MLB star. Did he have the dedication, the drive to spend long hours every day in the sun, perfecting his game and sweating it out on the field? Did he really have that sort of passion that burned bright in his belly?

He determined that wasn't the case. He loved baseball, but he didn't *live* for it. As for his son, Juan Jr, that wasn't true. In fact, even at an early age, it was becoming quite apparent that he had found a sport that he had fallen in love with and would follow for the rest of his life.

So, Juan Sr. didn't doubt his son just like he doubted himself. He saw a young star in the making. Even during those early baseball catch games in the front yard, Juan Sr. thought that something special was brewing inside his offspring.

He had little idea how far it would take him, though.

School, Family, Ball

Throughout the early years of his life, Juan spent days in school hanging out with friends and family, and then playing baseball. It was just that routine, again and again, day in and day out. Juan Sr. was very supportive of his son's budding talent and even Juan Jr. knew he was something special. He could sense that pride and excitement that other people close to him had when they watched him play.

He started his time on the baseball field in the very same place he would remain for many more years to come: in the outfield.

Playing in the baseball outfield is a difficult task that often isn't given the credit that it is due. Many people assume that playing in the outfield means you just stand around in the sun, the hat bill on your head blocking the rays above, and just wait. Wait for balls to roll out to you, wait for easy pop-flies that you can catch without breaking a sweat, or wait for the rest of the team's defense to do it all for you and the game's ending to meet you.

But that's simply not how it is. Playing in the outfield is hard work and it can be quite challenging because there are many variables. And there are also many differences between playing in the outfield and infield.

For example, those in the outfield are tasked with catching fly balls that reach a height of hundreds of feet before landing on their mitt. This is something that infielders don't need much practice or development with. That is because an infielder is typically going to catch line drives and grounders. They will instead focus on retrieving those, making tosses to the bases, and securing runners before they can get past them.

As for outfielders, they need to be able to predict, strategize, and conquer all sorts of balls and hits.

Juan quickly learned just how tricky and complicated playing in the outfield was. In many ways, the game really lives and dies on the work of the outfielders. Think of it this way: if an outfielder is on the ball—no pun intended—and is able to catch every ball that comes their way, then the game will go according to plan and their team will have an advantage until it's all over. But if an outfielder makes errors, doesn't communicate with others, or misreads a situation, then the game will decidedly go the wrong way for them.

There is a quiet tension for those playing in the outfield. At any moment, the baseball could come screaming out there and so much will be riding on it.

Juan quickly took to playing in the right field, which is complicated for a whole other reason. But Juan felt comfortable out there.

You may think that the games that Juan played at that age were easy, laid back, and stress-free. How hard can a game of school children really be? But you are not taking into consideration that this part of the world absolutely adores baseball and these young players are baseball fanatics and play at a level that is only a step or two away from the minor leagues.

Learning The Game

Juan was able to really perfect his abilities while playing in these games as a kid. He got better at catching; he got a whole lot better at batting and hitting the ball, as well as reading the pitcher. He also got much better and more efficient at communicating with other players on his team. He was quickly learning a language that only the very best baseball players master.

This is a language without words or phrases. This is a language about reading eyes, head nods, body language, and the little things that suggest someone's intentions without giving them away. It's a vital part of being a professional baseball player. If you have ever watched a game, you have seen this language between coaches and players, the pitcher and catcher, and anyone who wears a jersey.

In many ways, playing in these games as a youth was instructing and teaching Juan about the little intricacies of the game that cannot be laid out in a book. And it took his playing skills and style to a whole other level. His father, his brother and sister, his mother, and anyone who watched him play could see that Juan's talents were growing by leaps and bounds under the hot Dominican sun. Was he good enough to play in a minor league team? It was crazy to think that because he was barely a teen, but it wasn't outside the realm of possibility. A young, driven player like Juan Soto was the type that could ride a rocket to the minor league and beyond, even before he reached the legal drinking age.

Proving Himself: The Minor Leagues

As the years went on, Juan continued to play the game and continued to get much better at it. As he got closer and closer to his 20th birthday, it was time for him to decide if he wanted to take a shot at turning his passion for the game into a career in baseball. He had avenues he could follow. He had generated enough interest that he could attempt to become an unrestricted foreign free agent, as many other young men from his country had done in the past.

What would this do exactly? It would put him on the radar of scouts for the MLB. Unsurprisingly, they visited the DR every single year, hoping to find the next big thing. And they look under every rock, down every alley, and on every single baseball diamond. So, if Juan signed up to be a free agent, he would get some eyes on him.

Getting The Timing Right

But was it really the time for Juan to get that attention? He was surely doing terrific work on the field, out in the right field position that felt like home to him now. However, some self-doubt lingered. You wouldn't know it by watching Juan play. He performed with enthusiasm, ease, and confidence. In fact, he was already starting to become a playful and colorful character on the field. He was a few seasons away from perfecting his Soto Shuffle, but he was definitely a fired-up character during each and every game.

If Juan attempted to join the American minor league but wasn't quite ready, it could really set him back. He could tarnish his name and make himself known as the one who had too much confidence in himself. Getting to play baseball as a pro was something you had to do perfectly. You had to time it just right—not too early and not too late—in order to really find the right scout, the right agent, and the right team.

Juan was fearful that maybe he wasn't as good as he thought. Maybe he was in an echo chamber of family and friends who were praising him but were off base.

But he had to know for sure. He had to take a chance. The thought of missing out on playing baseball full time was just too frightening to this young man who had grown to love the game.

Juan took his chance and it paid off well. He was seen by the right scouts, got through the right try-outs, and, at such a young age, he was on his way to playing ball for a living. In July 2015, Soto agreed to terms with the Washington Nationals as an unrestricted foreign free agent.

This was obviously a huge accomplishment and got him much further than so many people before him had gone. It wasn't a sure thing to play baseball in the MLB, but it was certainly a huge and encouraging move.

Things could have still gone poorly for Juan after signing for the minor league. He could have sustained an injury or, perhaps even worse, gassed out and not live up to expectations. The young man was well aware that he hadn't "made it" because he had gained interest from an American minor league team.

His father told him as much, as did the other people who were close to him. They cautioned Juan that his signing to a minor league team wasn't the end of a long journey or the goal he was trying to meet. Instead, it was an opportunity. It was the first step to making it into the big leagues someday.

Now that he was in the minor leagues, Juan was going to be sent to a rookie-level affiliate team that was owned by the Washington Nationals. The game would be less attended and not on TV, and the competition and skills and talent wouldn't be on the same level with the MLB, but he would still be on track to playing with the big guys. Soto landed a role in 2016 with the Gulf Coast League Nationals and right off the bat he was one-upping other players, showing off his skills, and getting noticed by the people who mattered. Juan hit .368 with five home runs and 32 RBIs in his opening season in the minor leagues. These numbers were sure to drop a bit as he faced stiffer competition in the future, but they were a very promising start and were enough to earn him MVP honors.

THE NEXT LEVEL

Based on his work in his first season, it was no surprise that people had a lot of faith in Juan and wanted to move him up to a higher level of play, fame, and competitiveness. The powers that be wanted to kick his tires, lift his hood, and see if he really had what it took to go further than the minor leagues.

He was elevated to the Class A-Short Season New York-Penn League's Auburn Doubledays in September 2016 in time for the season's last few games. Anyone thinking that maybe the extra pressure would have a negative effect on Juan was quickly corrected. Although he had some difficulties, he showed that he could adjust to this newer, more intense level. He played with the Doubledays in six games, going 9 for 21 with three doubles and an RBI.

Beyond his talent, beyond his skill, the thing that really spoke to the fans and the people running these minor league teams was that Soto was a team player who was willing and eager to do whatever it took to secure a win. He was the sort of player who left his heart on the field and gave 110% every single time.

He was definitely very good at playing baseball, there was no doubt about that. Anyone could see that. But coaches within the minor leagues and also in the MLB saw that Soto was the sort of player who would work well with others and would do very well with direction and coaching. That is the sort of player that coaches want. That is the sort of player that other people want to play with. Really, that is the sort of player who can make a name for himself in the MLB and can become a vital part of any squad.

His rise to the top continued after his time with the Doubledays. In 2017, Juan was promoted again, this time to the Hagerstown Suns of the Class A South Atlantic League. This was the biggest stage yet for Juan and it would present him with his first serious setback in his young, aspiring baseball journey.

THE FIRST INJURY

Juan had a promising start to the season with the Suns until he suffered an ankle injury while sliding into home on May 2. He had played in 23 games with the Suns when he got hurt and was batting .360 with three home runs. For those who don't understand baseball, those are very good numbers and showed that Soto was perhaps about to have his best season yet. But the injury got in the way.

How an athlete deals with an injury says a lot about them. Do they accept it? Do they protest against the doctors and attempt to keep playing? Do they grow angry and irrational or calm and measured? Soto had never experienced an injury like this and wasn't sure how to act. He knew that a lot was riding on his career at this point. He had his heart set on playing in the MLB and that meant that he needed to play well and he needed to play well consistently. It didn't matter what drew him out of the games; if he wasn't on the field and wasn't making people notice him, then he wasn't going to keep moving up through the ranks of professional baseball in America.

Soto did not play for the Suns again in 2017 due to the injury, but thankfully, his career didn't come to a complete halt. He did have two rehab periods with Gulf Coast Nationals following his injury. The first of these rehabs lasted five games in July 2017 and the second lasted four games in September 2017. The purpose was to keep his wits and skills about him and to keep playing the game. It was a sign of belief from the team. They knew that Juan would be back once he got better.

This made Soto feel so much better about his first absence from the game. He felt like he was back on the right path and his future wasn't in jeopardy. But then, disaster struck again. On his road to full rehabilitation, Juan suffered a hamstring injury that ultimately forced him to miss the entire season. There would be no rehab periods after this injury. He was going to be out for the rest of the season, no questions asked. In some ways, it was good for Soto to be given this news. It made him come to terms with the reality of sitting out and allowed him to focus on getting better and not fighting against his body to do so prematurely. Before the injury took him out of contention, Juan went 8 for 25 in nine competitions with his team and concluded the 2017 campaign with a truly stellar batting average of .351, three home runs, and 18 RBIs.

The injury was not what he expected or wanted, and it was definitely a curveball that caught him off guard. But Juan also knew that he still had a lot of potentials and the MLB was surely waiting for him if he continued to play well—and avoid many more injuries.

Yes, the injury slowed him down but Major League Baseball was definitely taking notice of Soto and saw him as someone who could be easily crafted into a superstar in just a few years. There was no doubt that Juan was one of the best prospects in the minor levels going into 2018. He was the sort of outfielder who had a natural talent and an insistence on pushing and making himself a better athlete year after year. Soto also was showing his versatility even at a young age before reaching the MLB. There were scouts and coaching staffs all across the league who envisioned Soto as the sort of player who could be put in any spot on the line-up, even the most difficult ones, and he would soon excel. Yes, he was most comfortable as a right fielder, but there were many options ahead waiting for him.

Soto had shown how great he was in various teams throughout the minor leagues. He had committed to himself and the game. He was talented, he was driven, and he was having fun playing the game that he loved so much.

Just a few years before, Juan's father was one of the people who knew the talent his son had. But now he had quickly become one of the best MLB prospects in recent history. That meant that the final obstacles had been pulled away and the most important door had been opened: Juan Soto was about to enter the MLB.

THE BIG SHOW

Soto's hard-fought and challenging time in the minor leagues had paid off because he was about to take the last step on his pathway to Major League Baseball.

He had played for multiple teams, several of which were owned and operated by the Washington Nationals. They had kept a close eye on him during all those times and they were ready to finally move him to the highest honor: playing on the actual Washington Nationals team.

Therefore, on May 20, 2018, the Nationals promoted Juan to the major leagues for the first time to bolster their outfield following the absence of second baseman and outfielder, Howie Kendrick, because of injury. It is ironic that Juan's opportunity to join the MLB came because another player was facing an injury similar to his own.

Before being called up into the major league, Juan had already played in eight games for the Senators, going 10-for-31 with two doubles, two home runs, and 10 RBIs. Those games and statistics would be the last ones that Soto ever had in the minor leagues. He was onto bigger and better things.

For years, it was a solid fact that the Washington Nationals were one of the weaker teams in the MLB. But when Soto entered the squad, the team started to grow and move up, becoming a powerful force in the East. They actually had a chance to make it far into the playoffs for the first time in a long time. That means that Soto wasn't only joining the MLB; he was joining one of the more promising teams within it. Who could ask for more at such a young age?

He was so young that he was actually breaking MLB records with it. He was officially the first person born in 1998 to participate in a big league game, which was a fact that the media spoke about greatly before his big league debut. Soto played his first MLB game on May 20, 2018. The pressure was on, the crowd was loud, and Soto felt emotions, pressure, and gravity he had never experienced before. You can never quite explain the roar of the crowd of an arena until you are in the middle of it. Juan had played some big games throughout his short career. But playing for the Nationals at this level was something completely new, different, exciting, and, yes, a little frightening.

At Nationals Park in Washington, D.C., he entered the game as a pinch-hitter in the eighth inning against the Los Angeles Dodgers and was struck out swinging by relief pitcher, Erik Goeddel. Sure, it wasn't the start that Juan wanted for his first major league game, but right from the beginning, he was hooked on playing for the Nationals and performing for so many people. He struck out and yet he still felt amazing, calm, and invigorated. He could only imagine what the games ahead would feel like.

The team immediately got to work at testing Soto's versatility and seeing how great he was from anywhere on the field. In the following game, Soto started in left field for the first time in the major league versus the Padres at Nationals Park. On the first pitch of his first at-bat of the game, Soto connected for a 422-foot opposite-field, three-run home run off of Robbie Erlin. Soto walked back out to thunderous applause from the rabid spectators after crossing the bases and going back to the dugout. The fans were already hooked on his personality, style, attitude, skill, and the way he whipped himself around the bases. The cheers from the crowd proved to Juan that he was in the right place and that he could be there for a very long time.

Juan became the first adolescent to smash a home run in an MLB game since Bryce Harper did at age 19 in 2012. He also became the youngest player in team history to do so. After the game, Harper wildly praised his successor, saying Soto was "a special player."

He made his major league debut as a cleanup hitter on June 21 against the Baltimore Orioles. In a 4-2 triumph, he doubled home the winning run. Soto hit multiple home runs for the first time on June 13, 2018, against the New York Yankees. On June 29, 2018, against the Philadelphia Phillies at Citizens Bank Park, he accomplished the feat once more, contributing two home runs, four hits, and five RBIs to the Nationals' 17-7 victory over the Phillies. On September 11, 2018, Soto played the second game of a doubleheader against the Phillies, going 3-for-4 with four RBIs. On September 16, Soto broke Rickey Henderson's record of 20 years, 241 days by becoming the player to steal three bases in a single game at the age of 19 years, 326 days.

A GREAT START

He was obviously off to a great start in the MLB and was proving that he was very qualified to be playing at such a level. Juan Soto was on the radar of many MLB fans just days into his career and there were people all over the country praising the young man. He was definitely remarkably younger than most other people playing baseball, but his skills were much further ahead than anyone in his age bracket.

His age kept coming up again and again, but only for good reasons. In 414 at-bats in 2018, Soto was the youngest player in the National League and hit .292/.406/.517 with 79 walks, which was tenth in the National League, as well as 22 home runs and 70 RBIs.

He was doing so well that he was given an honor that set him apart from all the other newcomers in his league. Juan became the sixth player to get the honor three or more times when he was selected NL Rookie of the Month in June, July, and September. During the season, Soto broke a number of milestones for teenagers in MLB, including the most walks by a teen (he brought in 79), the most multi-home run games by a juvenile (three), the highest adolescent OBP (coming in at .406), and the highest teen OPS (.911). With his 22 home runs, Juan shared second place among teenagers with his former teammate, Bryce Harper. He also became the first adolescent to walk over 60 times in one baseball season plus an on-base percentage above .400.

Soto became the fourth player in MLB history to accumulate 100 extra-base hits before turning 21 on August 19, 2019. Later, he became the seventh MLB athlete ever to hit 30 home runs before turning 21 years old. In 2019, he batted .282/.401/.548 with 110 runs, 108 walks, 34 home runs, 110 RBIs, and 12 stolen bases in 13 attempts. He also ranked third in the league in walks with 108.

Juan was the first three-time Rookie of the Month winner to miss out on earning the National League Rookie of the Year title, placing in second place in the vote behind Braves outfielder, Ronald Acua Jr.

THE BIGGEST GAMES YET

Yes, he was winning a lot of praises and accolades, but his biggest challenge was ahead. The Washington Nationals were definitely performing well, partly because of the hard work that Juan was putting in. But even in Juan's wildest dreams, he didn't expect the Nationals to surge as far as they did in his opening season. As the season went on, their standing only got stronger and the chances of them actually making the World Series grew higher. That means that Juan, who still couldn't even legally drink in the United States, was on the verge of playing in the biggest baseball competition in the world.

How would you feel in that situation? Would you feel pressure beyond compare? Would you be too afraid to move? Would you second-guess yourself and assume you didn't have what it took? The anxiety associated with such success can paralyze someone. But that didn't happen to Juan. He felt ready for the challenge. It wasn't just because he believed in himself (even though he did and he was starting to really show his excitable personality on the field more, winning over even more fans), but it was because he also believed in his teammates and coaches and everyone associated with the Nationals. He knew their hearts, their drives, their desires. And because of that, he really felt they had a leg up on the rest of the competition.

He wasn't afraid of playing in the World Series. Instead, he was downright excited about it.

As the end of the season rapidly approached, it became very obvious that the Nationals were bound for the World Series. That meant that Juan Soto, who was still playing in the Dominican Republic just a few years before, was about to play in the World Series. He had come a long way in such a short amount of time.

In the days before clinching or losing a shot at the World Series, Juan thought back on the road that got him to that point. He remembered playing ball with his dad at home; he remembered falling in love with the game; he remembered becoming comfortable—even fanatical—about playing every day. He remembered the number of games he had to play back in the DR, fighting hard to break through all the other young talented stars in that country. And he especially remembered how it felt when he saw the progress being made and the attention he was receiving.

He had earned a spot in the World Series. The entire team had. Some people said he was too young to get that far that fast, but Juan knew most of those comments were made out of jealousy. He knew that when it came down to talent and the facts, he had proven himself.

The World Series

Sure enough, the Nationals were headed to the World Series, facing off against the fearsome and powerful Houston Astros, who had found success during the World Series recently. They were considered the best team in the league and they were going to make the lives of the Nationals very, very hard.

Soto wasn't worried, not in the slightest.

The World Series is a best-of-seven series. That means the first team to win four games wins the series and, therefore, wins the entire season. Juan knew he would have plenty of opportunities to prove himself, but he had to make each and every one count.

Surprising no one, that is exactly what he did. Soto became the fourth-youngest player in MLB history to ever smash a home run in a World Series when he launched a home ball off Houston Astros ace, Gerrit Cole, to open the fourth inning of Game 1. This was a huge achievement in any sort of game. But to do so in the World Series was a major moment that Juan would relish for the rest of his life. The fans went wild when Soto smashed that hit. If there were baseball fans who weren't paying attention to him before, they were certainly paying attention to him after that.

Years before, Juan's father Juan Sr. had made a prediction that his son would someday play in the World Series before he turned 21 years old. And Juan Jr. made his father proud. On October 25, Soto's 21st birthday, Game 3 of the World Series was played. There must have been some sort of birthday celebration before the game because Juan was beyond fired up for the game and played as if he had something to prove. It's rare for a player to achieve a home run in any MLB game but especially the World Series. But it's even particularly rare to do that more than once in said Series. Juan had already landed a home run in the first game of the series, but he wasn't done; he was going to do it yet again. Soto smacked yet another home run off Cole in Game 5 of the series, giving the Nationals their only run in a 7-1 defeat that dropped them to a deficit of 3 games to 2 in the best-of-seven series. You would think the young man wouldn't be able to hit another homer, especially against such a tough team, but that wasn't the case. The freshly-minted 21-year-old was at it again at the most important point of the series. Soto managed a third home run of the series, a game-winning solo home run off Justin Verlander in Game 6, to force a decisive Game 7.

In the end, it was Game 7 that decided their fate and made team history. The Nationals ended up winning the World Series, their very first one in team history. The streets of Washington, DC were wild with cheer and celebration and Juan Soto was beside himself with joy. Some athletes waited their entire careers to have a moment like that, showering in champagne as their team celebrated such a major win. The Washington Nationals were world champions. That meant that Juan Soto, hardly 21 years old, was also a world champion. He had achieved a life-long dream for many at such a young age. It was phenomenal, it was unheard of, it was a huge moment in his life and in his career. In fact, it left some wondering just where he could go next? How does someone top such an achievement?

The truth was that Juan didn't just play in the World Series; he *dominated* it. Some players just sit on the bench to play a little bit during the World Series. They might make an impact, but it is usually not a big one. That wasn't the case with Juan: he batted .277/.373/.554 in the postseason (as well as .333/.438/.741 in the World Series) with a mammoth five home runs and 14 RBIs. In fact, Soto was up front and led the Nationals in home runs, hits, walks, and runs scored throughout the series. Soto and Stephen Strasburg were later announced as co-winners of the 2019 Babe Ruth Award.

MOVING ON

The coronavirus pandemic ran rampant through the entire world after Soto and the Nationals' World Series win. It had an especially painful and troubling effect on the world of baseball, canceling games, causing many absences, and general uncertainty that threw multiple monkey wrenches into the works of the league.

It complicated Juan's career in some huge ways too, creating headaches and setbacks yet again for him. Soto tested positive for COVID-19 on July 23, 2020, prior to the second game of a condensed 2020 season. After many negative tests, Soto returned to competition on August 4. He admitted that he had been abiding by the team's social distance rules prior to the positive test, that he had never had COVID-19 signs, that he had obtained negative results on multiple tests the day prior to discovering the positive test result via the official MLB testing program, and that he thought the test that forced him to sit out the game was because of a false positive, which was quite common when people took COVID tests.

Juan was intent on starting off the season strongly and was upset that he was held back because of COVID. He had missed a few weeks of play because of the virus and he wanted to make up for the lost time. He was a champion now, an important part of the team, and one of the most loved up-and-coming stars in the MLB.

Right off the bat, Juan showed that he still had the ability and the drive to blast home runs. He was the reigning home run champion of the World Series because of the work he had done leading up to winning the championship, but Juan was ready to make homers a usual part of his regular career too.

Soto blasted two home runs in a series at Citi Field against the division rival, New York Mets, the first one measuring 463 feet on August 10 and the second one measuring 466 feet on August 12 to set a new best for himself. Following that, Juan received the distinction for the first time on August 17 as National League Player of the Week. That meant that just a little bit into his baseball career, he was already Rookie of the Month, a World Series champion, winner of the Babe Ruth award, and also the National League Player of the Week.

Juan proved that his first season wasn't a fluke as he continued to charge through the season. It was another great year for the young man. When it was all said and done, Soto had hit .351 throughout the regular season. On top of all that, Soto also had the greatest numbers in the three most important baseball categories for any big league player with at least 195 plate appearances in a season since Barry Bonds all the way back in the 2004 season. Soto was outpacing other guys who had been achieving success in the league for many years already. He surpassed all qualified hitters in MLB in on-base percentage, plus slugging percentage, as well as on-base plus slugging.

The awards and praise came pouring in for Juan after such a stunning impressive season. He already had the huge numbers; now he was due for some trophies too. Soto received both his first career Silver Slugger Award and his first career selection to the All-MLB First Team.

Juan was steadily building his career and seemingly getting better and better as he made his way through the MLB. In only a couple of seasons, he had already won the greatest honor in baseball and a number of other awards that set him apart from others in the league. Sadly, the Nationals failed to take advantage of Soto's excellent play, missing the playoffs.

2021 AND BEYOND

There was no doubt that Juan Soto was having an incredible baseball career, just a few years into his time with the Washington Nationals. However, some might wonder just what his goals were after doing so much in such a short amount of time. Where do you go when you have already climbed the highest mountain and achieved the biggest prize?

Soto was intent on continuing to play well and wanted to keep being one of the best, most pivotal guys on his squad.

So, when the 2021 season started, Juan was intent on improving his skills and doing more of the same, only better. Soto had a .313/.465/.534 batting line in 2021 with 29 home runs, 95 RBIs, and 111 runs scored.

The number of runs he scored was impressive because Juan Soto was making a name for himself as someone who really didn't swing on a lot of pitches. This wasn't done out of fear or because of a lack of skills. Instead, his reluctance to swing was because of strategy and a plan he had in mind to only swing when he knew he could hit the ball. It all made sense when you look at the game in an almost scientific sense. By swinging at an MLB-low 15.1 percent of pitches from outside the strike zone, he cemented his status as baseball's most methodical hitter. He was incredibly smart and able to read the pitcher and the balls they were throwing. He was sizing up the situation and he was saving his hits for the pitches he knew could result in hits and runs. So, in a very smart way, he was doing more by swinging less.

Juan's 145 total walks in 2021 made his season's total the greatest since Barry Bonds' 232 in 2004 when he broke the big league record. He was leaving the rest of the league in the dust statistically: Bryce Harper of the Philadelphia Phillies, a former teammate of Soto's, finished second in the league with 100 walks, making Soto the sixth player in the live ball era to have outpaced his league in walks by at least 40.

Juan ranked first in the major leagues for both deliberate walks (23 of them) and walk percentage (22.2%). He had the greatest walk-to-strikeout ratio in the majors. And throughout the season, he stayed committed to only swinging at the balls that he knew he could produce hits from. In fact, he only swung at 35% of pitches, which was the lowest proportion among major leaguers.

For his hard work and his great percentages, Soto received the National League Silver Slugger Award for the outfield and was selected to the All-MLB First Team after the season, earning both distinctions for the second consecutive year. He also came incredibly close to winning one of the biggest honors in baseball: Soto came in second place behind Bryce Harper in the vote for the National League Most Valuable Player Award. By doing so, Juan became the sixth MLB player in history to place second in the vote for both the MVP and Rookie of the Year awards. Sure, it didn't give him those ultimate honors but it was still wonderful to know how close he came to claiming them both.

What's Next For Juan Soto?

It is obvious that Juan Soto is a radically impressive, powerful, talented, and intelligent baseball player. He has done so much in just a few years. Think about all he has achieved since joining the league just out of his teenage years. How many people have had the honor of winning the World Series and so many awards and trophies? And how many of them are able to do so before they're 30, before they're even 25?

Beyond the winning record and the trophies, Juan Soto has done more than that: he has stayed true to himself and has found a legion of fans for himself because of his hard work, his attitude, his love of the game, and his dedication to always trying his hardest and doing his best. There are now millions of people all over the world who see the very same abilities that Juan's dad saw so many years ago back in the Dominican Republic.

His fans weren't just in the viewers of the game; it was in the management that ran his team. The Nationals attempted to extend Soto's contract by a massive 13 years and $350 million before the 2021–2022 MLB lockout, which would have locked up the then–23-year-old Soto until his 35th season in 2034. Soto turned down the offer, stating that he and his agent, Scott Boras, preferred to hold off on signing a deal until after the 2024 season when he would be a free agent. However, both Juan and his agent have repeatedly said that he considers Washington home and he wants to stick with the Nationals for years to come.

It wasn't the long deal that the team wanted but Soto and the Nationals reached an amicable $17.1 million contract on March 22, 2022, avoiding arbitration.

All of this means that the Nationals see Juan as the future of the team. The fact that they were attempting to sign him for such a long time only underscores that notion. As for Juan, he will possibly stick around with the Nationals for the rest of his career. But if he does, it won't be because other teams aren't trying to sign him. In fact, Juan is the sort of player that all the other teams in the league want. They want someone young; they want someone driven and talented and dedicated to the game. They want someone smart; someone who doesn't wildly swing at every single ball that comes his way.

Juan Soto has it all: talents, skill, smarts, and a drive to always do better.

Baseball is not an easy game. It requires some instincts and talents that aren't easy to come by. It takes years of training, hard work, and an insistence on never giving up. It's far more than just standing at home plate and waiting for a ball to fly to you so you can swing on it. It's not for everyone. And when you see someone who is really good at it, you need to remember just how much skill and work that player puts in every single swing.

Juan Soto is a young man, but he has already left his mark on the world of baseball. But he's not done—not even close. There is a good chance that fans of baseball will be watching Juan Soto swing, dance, and win for many, many years to come.

More From Jackson Carter Biographies

My goal is to spark the love of reading in young adults around the world. Too often children grow up thinking they hate reading because they are forced to read material they don't care about. To counter this we offer accessible, easy to read biographies about sportspeople that will give young adults the chance to fall in love with reading.

Go to the Website Below to Join Our Community

https://mailchi.mp/7cced1339ff6/jcbcommunity

Or Find Us on Facebook at

www.facebook.com/JacksonCarterBiographies

As a Member of Our Community You Will Receive:

First Notice of Newly Published Titles

Exclusive Discounts and Offers

Influence on the Next Book Topics

Don't miss out, join today and help spread the love of reading around the world!

Other Works By Jackson Carter Biographies

Patrick Mahomes: The Amazing Story of How Patrick Mahomes Became the MVP of the NFL

Donovan Mitchell: How Donovan Mitchell Became a Star for the Salt Lake City Jazz

Luka Doncic: The Complete Story of How Luka Doncic Became the NBA's Newest Star

The Eagle: Khabib Nurmagomedov: How Khabib Became the Top MMA Fighter and Dominated the UFC

Lamar Jackson: The Inspirational Story of How One Quarterback Redefined the Position and Became the Most Explosive Player in the NFL

Jimmy Garoppolo: The Amazing Story of How One Quarterback Climbed the Ranks to Be One of the Top Quarterbacks in the NFL

Zion Williamson: The Inspirational Story of How Zion Williamson Became the NBA's First Draft Pick

Kyler Murray: The Inspirational Story of How Kyler Murray Became the NFL's First Draft Pick

Do Your Job: The Leadership Principles that Bill Belichick and the New England Patriots Have Used to Become the Best Dynasty in the NFL

Turn Your Gaming Into a Career Through Twitch and Other Streaming Sites: How to Start, Develop and Sustain an Online Streaming Business that Makes Money

From Beginner to Pro: How to Become a Notary Public

Made in the USA
Las Vegas, NV
24 February 2025